SNAPSHOTS IN HISTORY

THE CHINESE REVOLUTION

The Triumph of Communism

by Paul J. Byrne

THE CHINESE REVOLUTION

The Triumph of Communism

by Paul J. Byrne

Content Adviser: Derek Shouba, History Professor
and Assistant Provost, Roosevelt University

Reading Adviser: Katie Van Sluys, Ph.D.,
School of Education, DePaul University

Compass Point Books ◈ Minneapolis, Minnesota

THE CHINESE REVOLUTION

 COMPASS POINT BOOKS

3109 West 50th Street, #115
Minneapolis, MN 55410

Visit Compass Point Books on the Internet at
www.compasspointbooks.com
or e-mail your request to
custserv@compasspointbooks.com

For Compass Point Books
Jennifer VanVoorst, Jaime Martens, XNR Productions, Inc.,
Catherine Neitge, Keith Griffin, and Carol Jones

Produced by White-Thomson Publishing Ltd.

For White-Thomson Publishing
Stephen White-Thomson, Susan Crean, Amy Sparks,
Clare Nicholas, Derek Shouba, Peggy Bresnick Kendler,
Will Hare, and Timothy Griffin

Library of Congress Cataloging-in-Publication Data
Byrne, Paul.
  The Chinese Revolution : the triumph of Communism / By Paul
Byrne.
      p. cm. — (Snapshots in history)
  Includes bibliographical references and index.
  ISBN-13: 978-0-7565-2006-9 (library binding)
  ISBN-10: 0-7565-2006-1 (library binding)
  ISBN-13: 978-0-7565-2012-0 (paperback)
  ISBN-10: 0-7565-2012-6 (paperback)
1. China—History—Civil War, 1945–1949—Juvenile literature. I.
Title. II. Series.

  DS777.54B96 2007
  951.04'2—dc22   2006027083

THE CHINESE REVOLUTION

CONTENTS

Meeting the Enemy

On August 28, 1945, a U.S. Army transport plane touched down in the remote Chinese city of Chongqing. Onboard was the Chinese Communist leader, Mao Tse-tung. The U.S. ambassador to China, Patrick Hurley, accompanied him. They had come to Chongqing for peace talks with the Chinese Nationalist leader, Chiang Kai-shek.

Mao and Chiang were longtime enemies. Their armies had battled each other on and off for more than 20 years. In the 1940s, the United States and much of the rest of the world recognized Chiang Kai-shek as the legitimate ruler of China. Mao Tse-tung, on the other hand, was considered a rebel. He had fought his way to the top of the Chinese Communist Party (CCP) and was its undisputed leader.

U.S. Ambassador Patrick Hurley (right) and Communist leader Mao Tse-tung got off the plane in Chongqing on August 28, 1945.

Unlike the citizens of the world's democratic nations, the Chinese Communists did not accept Chiang Kai-shek as the true leader of China. Although Chiang had tried for decades to destroy them, Mao and the CCP had managed to survive. By 1945, they ruled a large mountainous region in northern China and were trying to expand their control throughout the country.

When Chiang and Mao met for the peace talks, the future of China was as uncertain as ever. World War II had just ended two weeks earlier, when the Japanese surrendered to the United States and the Allies. The Japanese had conquered and ruled large parts of China and had long battled both the Nationalists and the Communists in many parts of the country. As a result, China was in ruins.

By the time the two rivals met in Chongqing, more than 10 million Chinese had died from war and starvation. Out of a population of around 600 million, nearly 100 million Chinese people

THE ALLIES

The World War II Allies were a group of more than 20 nations that worked together to defeat the Axis powers of Germany, Italy, and Japan. The Allies, which were led by the United States, Great Britain, and the Soviet Union, also included China. Because Chiang Kai-shek was the recognized leader of China, he was named supreme commander of the Allied forces in China, Burma, and India during the war.

roamed the country as refugees. With the war now over, the country was in a state of chaos, and the future of China was in question.

Chongqing was one city where the effects of war were easily seen. It was not a pleasant place to visit. Chongqing had become the most bombed city in history after the Japanese air force had spent years

The people of Chongqing suffered greatly during the war against Japan, as frequent bombings rained destruction on the city.

11

trying to destroy this base of Chinese resistance. The Japanese had set out to conquer China in 1937, which led to China's involvement in World War II and further bombing of China and its cities. Chongqing was overcrowded with war refugees and citizens who had fled the Japanese. In addition, it was polluted from the heavy manufacturing that had turned Chongqing from a small city into an industrial center during the war.

The Nationalists and Communists had stopped fighting each other in order to battle the Japanese when they invaded China, but the ongoing conflict now seemed certain to break out into a violent civil war. This was a war the United States wanted very much to prevent. After being allied against Japan with both the Nationalists and Communists in World War II, American leaders now wanted to see their Chinese allies work together to build a strong and united China.

Mao and Chiang agreed to talk peace, but the intense suspicion between the two leaders was clear from the moment Mao got off the plane in Chongqing. The Communist leader refused to ride in the official car Chiang had sent for him, likely fearing that it would be blown up with him inside. Mao instead rode from the airport with the U.S. ambassador. His flight to Chongqing was the first time Mao had flown in an airplane. It was also the first time he had journeyed from the safety of his mountain stronghold in nearly 10 years.

On the evening that Mao arrived, Chiang Kai-shek held a formal dinner to mark the occasion. In a large banquet hall decorated with banners and flowers, the two leaders stood eye to eye across the dinner table. They smiled at each other and raised their glasses in a toast. They toasted the Allied victory over the Japanese and the future of China. U.S. Ambassador Hurley looked on with approval. During dinner and at other occasions throughout his stay in Chongqing, Mao proclaimed to his audience, "Long live President Chiang Kai-shek."

Mao Tse-tung was a founding member of the Chinese Communist Party and rose to become its undisputed leader.

13

Behind the smiles and the words of kindness, however, both leaders were plotting against each other. In order to satisfy demands from Hurley and the other Americans, Chiang and Mao eventually agreed to share power and work together to build a new democratic government, but in reality both were interested in only one thing—complete control of China.

While Mao and Chiang discussed peace in Chongqing into the early autumn of 1945, their armies were on the move. In fact, they were already engaged in skirmishes and open battles in areas

*The Nationalist leader,
Chiang Kai-shek (right)
shared a toast with Mao Tse-
tungon the first night of their
peace talks in Chongqing.*

scattered across China. As much as the United
States wanted to stop a civil war from breaking out,
it seemed unavoidable.

Over the next four years, Mao's Communists
and Chiang's Nationalists would battle it out to
the bitter end. Eventually the Communists would
win control of China, and Chiang Kai-shek and the
Nationalists would be forced out of the country, to
the island of Taiwan. The hard-fought Communist
victory would not only decide the fate of the world's
most populated country. It would also shape the
future of Asia and the rest of the world. ◥

15

A Revolutionary Past

Chapter

2

Mao Tse-tung and Chiang Kai-shek started out as allies. A revolution had swept through China in October 1911, when Chiang and Mao were both young men. Chiang was already a trained military officer and fought in the 1911 Revolution. Mao was a student who quit his studies to join the revolution.

The 1911 Revolution brought about the downfall of the Chinese Empire, which had ruled China for more than 2,000 years. The empire had grown weak in its old age. The Chinese economy was by then largely under the control of powerful foreign nations such as France, Great Britain, the United States, and Japan. These nations were known as the imperialist powers, and they controlled many of the seaports and other large cities in China.

During the 1911 Revolution, Chinese students and others gathered in mass demonstrations. Many young people cut off their traditional ponytails to protest the old ways of China.

This foreign domination of China angered many Chinese and led directly to the 1911 Revolution and the collapse of the empire.

One of the main leaders of the revolution was Sun Yat-sen. Sun and others wanted to create a modern democratic form of government to replace the empire that had ruled China for so long. By fighting for democracy in China, Sun Yat-sen inspired patriotism in many of his countrymen and became a heroic figure in much of the country. Sun formed a political party called the Kuomintang to serve in the new government. The Kuomintang, (KMT), was also known as the Nationalist Party.

Revolutionary leader Sun Yat-sen was inspired by the Founding Fathers of the United States, and became known as the George Washington of China.

Chiang Kai-shek became a close friend of Sun Yat-sen's and a key leader in the Nationalist Party. Unfortunately for the Nationalists, their plans for a democratic China never came true. The Republic of China, which was formed after the 1911 Revolution, quickly fell apart as military warlords carved China up into their own personal kingdoms. These warlords were military leaders who had served in the emperor's army.

With the empire gone, many of these warriors preferred to rule their own regions of China rather than obey the central government of the new republic. Despite the rule of warlords throughout China, Sun Yat-sen and the Nationalists were determined to reunite the country and establish a lasting modern government.

Meanwhile, after the revolution, Mao Tse-tung returned to his studies and eventually became interested in the theories of communism. In July 1921, Mao and a dozen or so men met in an abandoned factory in the city of Shanghai. There they created the Chinese Communist Party (CCP).

The CCP was supported by the Soviet Union, the Communist government formed in Russia after the Russian Revolution of 1917. The Soviet Union also supported Sun Yat-sen and the Nationalists, which led to an alliance between the two Chinese parties. Their common goal was to stage a new revolution to defeat China's warlords and unite China under a single government.

With assistance from the Soviets, a military academy was founded in southern China, and recruits were trained to be disciplined military officers. Chiang Kai-shek was the academy's first commander, and in 1925 he founded the National Revolutionary Army to challenge the warlords who ruled China.

While Chiang was building his army, Mao was stationed in the countryside among the villages of Hunan, his home province. As in other parts of China, most people in Hunan were peasants. Peasant uprisings were common at that time, and massive peasant rebellions had overrun the country in the past. As a representative of the CCP, Mao's aim was to organize this power of the peasant masses into a new revolution in China. The future Communist leader predicted:

> *Several hundred million peasants will rise like a mighty storm, like a hurricane, a force so swift and violent that no power, however great, will be able to hold it back.*

COMMUNISM

Communism is an economic system based on government ownership of property and sharing of property and resources evenly among all members of a society. German economist Karl Marx, who wrote about communism, predicted that communism would overtake capitalist societies, as existed in Germany. He theorized that urban industrial workers would seize control by revolting against factory owners and other capitalists. Mao Tse-tung knew that China was nothing like Germany. China's workers were overwhelmingly rural peasants. So Mao's version of communism called for the rural peasants to revolt against landowners.

By 1926, Chiang's National Revolutionary Army was a well-trained military force. Sun Yat-sen had died, and Chiang Kai-shek became the main leader of the Nationalist-Communist alliance. With an army of 100,000 trained and eager troops, Chiang set out from his base in southern China to conquer the warlords who ruled most

As head of the Whampoa Military Academy, Chiang Kai-shek became the leader of the National Revolutionary Army, and soon became the leader of the Nationalist Party as well.

21

of the country. Within two years, Chiang's military campaign, which became known as the Northern Expedition, was a huge success, since many of China's warlords either had been defeated or had agreed to join a national government.

As Chiang strengthened his control over China, he grew concerned about his Communist allies. Chiang and others feared that the mass peasant uprisings and other violence being promoted by the Communists might threaten the country's new national government. Tensions arose between the two parties, and Chiang eventually decided it was time to end his partnership with the Communists.

The alliance came to a violent end in April 1927, when Chiang turned his forces against a Communist-led worker's uprising in China's largest industrial city, Shanghai. Thousands of workers and CCP members were killed in what became known as the Shanghai Massacre. From this moment on, Mao Tse-tung and other Communists became outlaws, and Mao and Chiang became enemies.

After breaking his alliance with the CCP, Chiang formed a national Chinese government with its capital in the eastern city of Nanjing. Chiang and his Nationalists were now seen by many Chinese as the rightful leaders of all China. The Chinese people felt a new surge of patriotism because they now had a national government that promised to unify the country. The Nationalists made diplomatic and economic treaties with the foreign imperialists, who

had maintained their power in China throughout the warlord era. Most of these countries now agreed to recognize Nationalist authority in China.

Over the following years, the Nationalists made many political and economic reforms, and China seemed headed for a brighter future. In actuality, however, the future would instead bring misery and warfare unlike anything the country had ever known. ◣

Thousands fled Hankou as Chiang's army approached the city during fighting between the Nationalists and Communists.

From Outlaws to Conquerors

Chapter

3

While Nationalist government officials worked to secure control over Chinese society, Chiang Kai-shek continued to build up the National Revolutionary Army. His main goal was to hunt down his former allies—the Chinese Communists. Chiang now considered the Communists to be the most dangerous threat to the new China the Nationalists were building.

After the Shanghai Massacre, the surviving Chinese Communists were scattered throughout the country, and several CCP bases were created in remote areas that still remained outside of Chiang's control. Mao Tse-tung survived as the leader of a small rebel army and eventually joined forces with other Communist leaders. In the early 1930s, Mao and the military leader Zhu De, a former warlord, built an army of 80,000 soldiers and controlled an area in southeastern China about the size of the state of New York.

This Communist army was a ragtag group of displaced city dwellers, local recruits, wandering

The Nationalist army was often on the march in its fight against Communists.

25

bandits, and former Nationalist soldiers who switched sides when the alliance split apart. They called themselves the Red Army because red is the symbolic color of communism, and Communist armies carry red flags into battle. The Red Army battled Chiang's forces and won small victories.

In the fall of 1934, Chiang sent his largest force yet to fight the Communists. More than 250,000 Nationalist troops surrounded an area located in the provinces of Jiangxi and Fujian that was controlled by the CCP. The Red Army's only hope was to break through the Nationalist blockade and try to escape. In October 1934, roughly 100,000 Communist troops and civilians battled their way through Nationalist lines and began a retreat that would take them on the longest journey of their lives. Their journey became known as the Long March.

During the Long March, the Red Army retreated across China before joining with another Communist army in the northern region of Yenan. Mao's army marched 6,000 miles (9,600 km) in a little more than one year. Chiang Kai-shek's forces chased them throughout most of the journey. In addition, Mao's army battled hostile tribes as they crossed the barren frontiers of China. Of the 100,000 people they started with, only about 15,000 survived the march. About 85 percent of the marchers died from battles, starvation, or exposure to the elements. As one Long Marcher recalled:

We finished all our food, so we dug up wild grass and peeled bark off trees. We even took off our belts and cooked them with a little salt. And we survived.

The dramatic stories and legends that arose out of the Long March led many in China to view Mao and the Communists as heroes. And so Mao Tse-tung was able to turn this military defeat into a personal victory. Mao went from being a radical outsider among the CCP leaders to the supreme leader of both the CCP and the Red Army.

After the Long March, Mao Tse-tung (center) became the undisputed leader of the Chinese Communists. Chou En-lai (left) was his second in command, and Zhu De was the commander in chief of the Red Army.

Chiang remained determined to destroy the Communists and continued to order attacks against them. But while Chiang was focused on defeating the CCP, an enemy much more powerful than Mao and his Communists was preparing for a confrontation. Japan had kept military forces in northern China and had seized control of the northern region of Manchuria in the early 1930s. In 1937, the Japanese launched an all-out war against China and invaded the heartland of the country.

This Japanese invasion of China marked the beginning of a long war between the two nations known as the Sino-Japanese War. Chiang was forced to give up his fight against the Communists and instead join them in trying to defend China from Japanese assaults. Unfortunately for the Chinese, Chiang's Nationalist forces were overwhelmed and defeated by powerful Japanese armies. The Nationalist government in Nanjing was forced to flee deep inside China, all the way back to the city of Chongqing.

The Japanese were building an empire in East Asia, and their conquest of China was only the first step. This military aggression was opposed by the United States and Great Britain, both of which had huge economic interests in China and East Asia and wanted to prevent Japanese domination of the region.

The United States began to send aid to Chiang and the Nationalists soon after the Japanese

invasion. American military pilots were recruited to battle the Japanese. Chiang Kai-shek and the Nationalists continued to gain support from the U.S. government as the United States and Japan drifted toward war.

Even before the Sino-Japanese War, Japanese forces occupied parts of China. Japanese troops marched through the streets of Shanghai in the early 1930s.

On December 7, 1941, the Japanese attacked the American naval base at Pearl Harbor in Hawaii. The next day, the United States declared war against Japan, and the war between the Chinese and Japanese now became part of World War II. Both Chiang's Nationalists and Mao's Communists were now allied with the United States against Japan.

29

Nationalist soldiers guarded American P-40 fighter planes based in China. The planes were flown by a group of elite American combat pilots known as the Flying Tigers.

Since the end of the Long March, Mao and the Communists had survived in the mountainous region around the city of Yenan, where they gradually rebuilt their military forces. Unlike the Nationalists, who tried to fight the Japanese in head-on battles, the Communists relied on ambushes and hit-and-run attacks against the invaders. The CCP was able to stage attacks in areas controlled by the Japanese and to disrupt the enemy's supply lines. Their efforts earned the Communists much prestige during the war years.

While the Japanese pushed the Nationalists out of eastern China during the war, the Communists were able to expand their control to areas beyond their mountain stronghold in and around Yenan. In the areas they controlled, the CCP seized land from owners and turned it over to the peasant farmers. These so-called land reforms earned the Communists support among the peasants who acquired the land.

Even though Mao and Chiang were supposed to be allies during the war against Japan, their forces spent more time fighting each other than they did cooperating with each other against the Japanese. The Nationalists fiercely opposed the CCP's land reforms and took lands back from CCP control wherever they could. More important, both leaders could see that the United States would eventually defeat Japan and that China would be liberated. So instead of working together, Mao and Chiang prepared themselves for their coming battle to control China.

The problem for Chiang was that while the Communists had grown stronger during the war against Japan, his Nationalists had lost much of their power and prestige in China. By the time World War II was nearing its end in 1945, the Communists were no longer retreating from the Nationalists—they were instead challenging them for control of China. ◣

The Communists Invade Manchuria

Chapter

4

While the Americans were trying to secure a peace deal between Mao and Chiang in Chongqing throughout September 1945, CCP and Nationalist military forces continued moving into the areas of eastern China being surrendered by the Japanese. The goal of both Mao and Chiang was to gain control of Manchuria in northeastern China.

This large territory north of China's Great Wall was the most economically important part of the country. Manchuria was where much of the industry in China was located. The region contained many natural resources, such as coal, iron, and forests. After they conquered Manchuria, the Japanese had turned it into its own country and renamed it Manchukuo.

On August 9, 1945, just a few weeks before Mao flew to Chongqing and just a few hours before the United States dropped a second atomic bomb on Japan, the armies of the Soviet Union attacked

The Great Wall of China was built in ancient times to stop northern invaders from attacking the heartland of China.

Japanese forces in Manchuria. The Soviets quickly overran the entire region.

U.S. leaders had been looking forward to the Soviet attack because they thought it would help the Allies defeat the Japanese. But once the Japanese surrendered, the Soviets and Americans began to see each other as enemies, not only in China, but also in Europe, where the Allies had worked together to defeat Nazi Germany. The United States and its Western allies now saw communism as the biggest threat to the world. This growing rivalry at the end of World War II marked the beginning of the Cold War.

The Soviet invasion of Manchuria was very good news for Mao and the CCP. They already had a close relationship with the Communist government of the Soviet Union and could now look to the Soviets to help them gain control of

THE COLD WAR

The Cold War is the name given to the long era of hostility and military struggle between Western capitalist nations, led by the United States, and those that practiced some form of communism, led by the Soviet Union. The Soviet Union supported communist armies in many parts of the world, while the United States wanted to stop the spread of communism and supported struggling capitalist nations. Western leaders saw communism as a threat to people's freedoms as well as free trade and capitalist economies. Though the civil war in China had begun long before the Cold War, China now became one of the first battlegrounds of the Cold War.

China. This is what leaders in the U.S. military and government started to fear once the Japanese surrendered. The Americans supported Chiang Kai-shek as the leader of China and did not want to see any more of the country fall into the hands of Mao and the Communists.

Shortly after Japan surrendered, a force of 50,000 U.S. Marines quickly moved into China to seize control of Beijing, the former capital of the Chinese Empire. They also occupied the nearby seaport of Tianjin, so the Communists could not capture these two important cities. American commanders instructed the defeated Japanese to surrender only to the Nationalists and not to the Communists.

From their base in the north of China, however, Mao's Communists were closer to Japanese-held areas in northeastern China than the Nationalists were in distant Chongqing and southern parts of the country. To overcome this enormous distance, U.S. military ships and aircraft rapidly transported thousands of Chiang's soldiers to eastern China to retake control from the Japanese. But CCP forces were able to move into many areas faster than the Americans could transport Nationalist armies. This was especially true in Manchuria, where the Soviets welcomed their Communist comrades.

All this was happening while Mao and Chiang and the Americans were still talking peace in Chongqing. A deal between the two leaders was finally signed on October 10, 1945.

As soon as Mao Tse-tung arrived back at his base in Yenan, he immediately returned to planning for war against the Nationalists. The agreement he and Chiang had made to share power was meaningless, and both leaders knew it. Instead of working together toward a united China, Communists and Nationalists were now fighting wherever they met.

Mao Tse-tung focused on the coming battle for Manchuria. Knowing that this strategically important region was the key to controlling all of China, the Communist leader promised his followers, "If we have Manchuria, our victory will be guaranteed."

Leading the Communists in Manchuria was Mao's most trusted military commander. General Lin Biao

General Lin Biao became the Communists' top battlefield commander.

was a legendary warrior who had been fighting with the Communists since he was 16 years old. He became a commanding officer before the age of 20, and it was believed that he had never lost a battle.

General Lin led a force of more than 50,000 men into Manchuria, where they seized areas not already controlled by the Soviets. Once they were there, Lin's army was joined by thousands of militia fighters scattered among the civilian population. Many of these guerrillas were ordinary civilians who had remained undercover CCP agents during the war with Japan and who now helped the Communists take control of their towns and villages.

While Lin's army grew in the north, Nationalist forces began pouring back into the heartland of China south of the Great Wall. Chiang still had many more troops under his command than Mao, and some of his armies were trained and equipped by the United States. Despite their greater numbers, better training, and weapons, Chiang's armies found that as long as the Soviet troops were there, they could not move into Manchuria to challenge the Communists.

COMMUNIST GUERRILLAS

Guerrillas are groups of lightly armed soldiers who fight a stronger enemy with stealth and ambushes rather than in large, open battles. Chinese Communist guerrillas came in many forms. Some were peasants formed into village defense units. Others became underground Communists in towns and cities and engaged in spying and sabotage. Even the Red Army itself was made up of units that often fought as guerrillas rather than as a regular army.

Soviet forces stayed in Manchuria many months after the end of World War II and secretly aided the CCP.

The Soviets had promised the Allies they would leave Manchuria soon after Japan surrendered and that they would return conquered land to the Nationalists. But they were not living up to their agreement.

While Soviet troops remained in Manchuria, Lin's army built up its strength. Even though Soviet leaders agreed to support the Nationalists as the government of China, Soviet commanders secretly turned over captured Japanese weapons to CCP forces. These included machine guns, artillery, battle tanks, and aircraft. They even handed over Japanese prisoners of war, who trained the Communists to use the seized Japanese weapons.

In addition to these Japanese prisoners, Lin was given command of more than 200,000 well-trained Chinese soldiers who had served as the native army of Japanese-controlled Manchukuo.

With all the help from the Soviet Union and the addition of the Manchukuo soldiers, Lin saw his army of less than 100,000 grow into a force that numbered close to 500,000 by the end of 1945. It looked as though the Communists were in Manchuria to stay. ◣

Marshall's Mission

Chapter

5

Halfway across the world, in Washington, D.C., U.S. President Harry Truman and his administration were growing increasingly worried about the situation in China. As the Communists grew stronger throughout northern China, the Soviets continued to arm them in Manchuria. At the same time, American leaders began to fear that Chiang and the Nationalists could lose the whole country to the Communists. The United States, however, still believed it could stop the civil war from growing out of control and that a Nationalist-led government could rule China.

By late November 1945, U.S. Ambassador Patrick Hurley had grown frustrated with the failure of both sides to maintain the truce they had agreed to in Chongqing. Hurley also complained that other American diplomats, as well as some American leaders at home, were giving up on Chiang and the Nationalists and that some were even supporting the Communists. Some leaders in the U.S. Congress were calling for an end to American involvement in China altogether. They feared the United States would be drawn into the civil war. Frustrated and angry, Ambassador Hurley resigned on November 27, 1945.

On that same day, President Truman handed a new assignment to one of the most respected leaders of the day. General George Marshall had been the top military leader of U.S. forces during World War II. The 64-year-old general had just arrived home for a well-deserved rest when he

General George C. Marshall went from being supreme U.S. military commander during World War II to the top U.S. diplomat after the war.

got a phone call from the White House. It was the president asking him to be his special representative in China. Marshall dutifully accepted his mission.

General Marshall could see that his task, finding a peaceful solution in China, would be difficult. When he arrived in China in December 1945, he was filled in on the situation by the top American commander in the country. General Albert Wedemeyer gave Marshall a gloomy report, warning that the civil war was growing and could not likely be stopped. But Marshall was not the kind of man to give up easily. He told Wedemeyer, "I'm going to accomplish my mission and you're going to help me."

Despite Marshall's determination to halt the civil war, the two sides seemed just as determined to carry on their battle. The Nationalists managed to land an army on the northeast coast near the Great Wall, and they soon pushed the Communists out of the area. Chiang now focused on building up

THE NEGOTIATOR

General George C. Marshall served under President Franklin D. Roosevelt as military chief of staff during World War II. After serving as the leader of the entire American war effort, he went on to become a world diplomat. After Truman became president and the war ended, Marshall was a negotiator for a number of post-war conflicts, including the conflict in China. He went on to become President Truman's secretary of state and launched the Marshall Plan, which successfully rebuilt the war-torn nations of western Europe.

Nationalist strength for a massive attack north into Manchuria.

Meanwhile, the Nationalists had not yet secured control in the rest of eastern China south of the Great Wall. In fact, while Chiang's forces battled in the north, the CCP was building another army farther south in the eastern province of Shandong. This put Mao's forces closer to China's heartland and the base of Nationalist power.

With the fighting getting out of control and spreading to new areas of China, Marshall demanded a cease-fire. He called on both sides to resume peace talks. He met with Chiang and other Nationalist leaders, along with Chou En-lai, who had long served as the CCP's representative in Chongqing. By the middle of January 1946, Marshall had persuaded the two sides to agree on a new truce. Like previous truces between these two enemies, however, it did not last long.

Chou En-lai was a Communist diplomat who agreed to the cease-fire of 1946.

43

In early March 1946, the moment Chiang had been waiting for arrived. The Soviets started withdrawing their forces from Manchuria. As the Soviets were leaving, some of Chiang's best-trained soldiers quickly moved in to attack CCP forces, who suddenly did not seem as tough as they did with the Soviets protecting them. Even with the help of the Soviets and the local Chinese forces, the Communist army in Manchuria was still inferior to Chiang's elite forces. The Nationalists quickly conquered the cities of southern Manchuria and forced the Communists to retreat north.

Despite Marshall's objections, Chiang continued to violate the truce and battle against the Communists in Manchuria. His forces fought their way north along the main railroad, and within three months they controlled all but one major city in northern Manchuria. At this crucial time, when it looked as if Chiang was turning the tide against the Communists, Marshall demanded a cease-fire. The American general insisted that it was his mission to bring peace to China.

By early June 1946, Chiang gave in to Marshall's demands and called off his

SOVIET WAR BOOTY

When the Soviets withdrew from Manchuria, they took huge amounts of industrial machinery back to the Soviet Union. Whole factories were uprooted, their pieces put on trains and shipped north. In all, the Soviets seized more than $3 billion of materials, which they tried to justify as war booty, or compensation for damages during the war. They made this claim even though it was the Germans who caused most of the losses the Soviets suffered in World War II.

attacks in Manchuria. Chiang felt forced to do what Marshall asked because the United States supplied the Nationalists with money and arms, both of which Chiang needed to fight the Communists. Marshall threatened to cut off this support from the United States if Chiang did not stop the fighting.

This time, the cease-fire lasted less than one month. By early July 1946, Chiang had launched new attacks all over northern China. Marshall was furious. He ordered a stop to U.S. aid to China. Although he stayed involved in Chinese affairs through the rest of the year, Marshall was beginning to understand that his attempts to find peace were hopeless.

Marshall spent much of the late summer in 1946 with Chiang and his wife at their summer home. Madame Chiang Kai-shek had become a major diplomat for the Nationalists. She was educated in the United States and spoke fluent English. She had traveled to the United States during the war to build support for China, and was the first Chinese citizen to address the U.S. Congress. During the war, Madame Chiang and her husband had become one of the most famous married couples in the world.

Despite his efforts, throughout his extended stay with the Chiangs, Marshall could not persuade the Nationalist leader to halt attacks against the Communists. The general's mission to China would be one of the few failures of his long and celebrated career. ◣

45

The Hearts and Minds of the People

Chapter

6

Most ordinary Chinese citizens feared and despised the growing civil war. They were sick and tired of the fighting. Whether they lived in the crowded cities along China's coasts or tiny villages in the countryside, people simply wanted to see their lives get better after suffering through so many years of war. Most Chinese would probably have agreed with Marshall that the two sides needed to come together to save their country from chaos and start building a better future.

The Nationalist Party had been trying to guide China toward its future for some time. Before the war with Japan, it had strong support in the cities along China's coasts, where people had the most contact with the outside world and the most experience with democracy. During the

Nationalist Chinese soldiers marched in Shanghai while the Communist army strengthened its forces in the nearby countryside.

early days of Nationalist rule, people enjoyed more freedoms than ever. But the Japanese invasion put an end to any progress the Nationalists had made in China and destroyed much of the support they held in the cities.

Chinese politics were focused mostly on China's cities. Most peasants living in the countryside knew little, if anything, about national politics. The world they knew was limited to farms and the villages where they lived. Many of China's peasants spent their entire lives working on small farms they did not own. The little money they earned was used to pay rent and taxes to powerful landowners, who in turn controlled their lives. Many of the landlords abused their poverty-stricken tenants.

LANDLORDS

In the mid-1900s, Chinese landlords owned huge areas of land. Peasants lived and worked on the land and paid rent to a landlord. Some landlords had their own personal militias to enforce their will over the local peasants. It had been this way since the days of the Chinese Empire.

Throughout his life as a revolutionary, Mao Tse-tung had learned to take advantage of the social injustices in China's rural areas. He called on peasants to rebel against their landlords and seize their lands and property. In the areas they controlled, the CCP imposed land reforms, which were designed to destroy the Chinese system of landlords. As they conquered new areas during the civil war, the Communists brought land reforms with them.

Once the CCP was in control of an area, Communist agents known as cadres entered the villages. A typical farming community was home to dozens of peasant families living in small homes made of brick, wood, or mud. The homes were connected by dirt roads winding through the village. The Communists ordered large meetings of the whole population of a village, including women and children. Cadres used these meetings to instruct villagers in the ways of Mao's communism. They promised that land reforms would improve the peasants' lives and told them the land they once rented now belonged to everyone in the village.

CCP forces often captured local landlords and their families, who were then brought into the villages for "people's trials." The landlords faced

Peasants throughout China burned their landowners' property deeds.

49

charges of abuse from their former tenants. A village leader from Shanxi Province recalled the trial of the local landlord named Jinghe:

> *Old women who had never spoken in public before stood up to accuse him. … Altogether over 180 [accusations] were raised. Jinghe had no answer to any of them. He stood there with his head bowed. We asked him whether the accusations were false or true. He said they were all true. … That evening, all the people went to Jinghe's courtyard to help take over his property.*

After confessing to any wrongs they may have committed, landlords were often brutally tortured and beaten to death by vengeful peasants. The Communists allowed and encouraged this violence. In fact, Mao's version of land reform often called for the murdering of landlords and seizing of their land. Troops joined peasants in looting the landlords' estates and dividing food supplies and other property among themselves.

It was not always abusive landlords who were robbed and murdered. In some villages, families were targeted just because they were a little better off than their neighbors, or simply because their neighbors did not like them. Many innocent people were accused of being landlord sympathizers, and untold thousands were terrorized and murdered.

By tapping into the anger and violence of China's poorest people, Mao turned masses of them into Communist supporters. All over northern China,

CCP-led peasant militias grew larger. The new recruits expanded the ranks of the Red Army, which Mao renamed the People's Liberation Army (PLA), so they would seem less like conquerors and more like liberators.

While the PLA built its strength among peasants in rural parts of China, Chiang Kai-shek and the Nationalists were failing to re-establish the support they once held in the cities. When the Nationalists regained control of economic centers such as Tianjin and Shanghai from the Japanese, they imposed harsh taxes on citizens and businesses. Many jobs were lost after Japanese-run businesses left, and government officials could not seem to get the economy rolling again. To make things worse, the Chinese currency rapidly lost its value, and whatever money people had was soon nearly worthless.

Unfortunately, some of the Nationalist officials were corrupt and profited from their positions of power. It seemed that government officials and those close to them were the only ones living well inside the cities they controlled, and average citizens resented them for it. Some people were so upset by

INFLATION

Inflation occurs when currency loses its value. After World War II and during the civil war, the Chinese currency, called the *yuan,* declined in value so much that it became almost worthless. As the yuan declined in value, more of it was needed to buy anything. For example, a bag of flour that had once cost around 45 yuan exploded in price to 50 million yuan. People's financial lives were destroyed, and many people lost their life savings.

51

Nationalist corruption and incompetence that they were driven to support the CCP. Some even joined the Communist underground in their towns and cities.

By early 1947, Chiang knew that he was losing the battle for the hearts and minds of the Chinese people. He needed a dramatic victory over the Communists to boost the morale of his supporters. He decided to attack Yenan, where Mao and other top CCP leaders had their headquarters. In the spring of 1947, he ordered one of his top generals, Hu Ysung-nan, to lead the assault against Yenan.

Hu and an army of 250,000 Nationalists marched to Yenan, only to find the city abandoned. With most of his men fighting in eastern provinces, Mao only had about 20,000 troops nearby to protect his base. Rather than pulling his armies back to defend Yenan, as Chiang Kai-shek hoped he would, Mao and other CCP leaders simply disappeared into the surrounding mountains before the Nationalists arrived.

As Nationalist forces searched the area for rebels over the following months, they were repeatedly hit by deadly ambushes. The whole campaign turned into a disaster. It was as if the PLA knew their enemy's every move and were always a few steps ahead of them. It was even suspected that the Nationalist commander, Hu, was a Communist spy working for Mao.

The capture of Yenan was failing to give Chiang

Kai-shek the symbolic victory he needed. His standing with the Chinese people continued to decline. At the same time, Mao's ability to avoid capture and score military victories, as well as stories of the Red Army stealing from the rich and giving to the poor, made the Communist leader more popular than ever. ◣

Most of the citizens remaining in the city of Yenan after the Communists abandoned their capital were women, children, and the elderly.

Decisive Battles

Chapter

7

Chiang Kai-shek traveled to Yenan soon after Hu's army took over the city. News cameras were there to give the illusion of Nationalist success. Chiang wanted to show the rest of China that the Nationalists had been victorious in conquering the CCP.

The cameras filmed the Nationalist leader marching through the deserted Communist base. Chiang and his entourage were shown caves carved into the nearby mountainsides where the CCP had survived years of bombing raids by the Japanese and the Nationalist air force. At first, the newsreels of Chiang's tour helped spread rumors of Mao Tse-tung's capture or death.

But the Communist leader quickly emerged from hiding to broadcast radio messages to his

Nationalist troops had more firepower than the Communists.

armies and supporters. Mao told them to carry on their fight wherever they were. He thought of the capture of Yenan as only a distraction from important battles elsewhere in China.

While Chiang was trying to make the capture of Yenan into a victory for the Nationalists, his army was in serious trouble in Manchuria. The Communist Red Army, under General Lin Biao's command, had been on the run until Marshall's cease-fires. But now it had regrouped in the far northern city of Harbin. The Red Army was well established there and had created a defensive line that the Nationalists could no longer break.

The Communists now had a secure base that shared borders with the Soviet Union and North Korea. Both countries were friends of the CCP, and both countries supplied them with weapons and new recruits.

Nationalist soldiers battled Communist forces in Manchuria.

During the winter months of 1947, Communist troops crossed the ice of the Sungari River in northeast China to launch counterattacks against Chiang's Nationalists on the other side. Lin's troops were hardened against the bitter cold Manchurian winter. They raided Nationalist bases at Changchun and other cities. The Red Army inflicted heavy casualties while capturing tons of weapons and whole cargo trains full of supplies from the Nationalists.

Even though they were still able to fight off the Communists by using their superior firepower, Nationalist commanders in the northern cities began to fear their supply lines to the south would be cut off completely. Once cut off from their suppliers in the south, they knew their armies would become trapped.

The Nationalists relied on the main railroad connecting the major cities. However, long stretches of the railroad crossed through remote rural areas where Communist militias remained in control.

RAILROADS

The railroads of China were extremely important to the Nationalists as they tried to maintain control of China. The vast majority of the country was undeveloped farmland without highways or even paved roads. Therefore, Nationalist armies had to rely heavily on railroads to transport troops and equipment.

Even if the Nationalists drove the regular Red Army troops out of the cities and away from the rail lines, Communist militias were never far away in the surrounding villages.

Throughout 1947, the civil war continued to turn in Mao's favor. Hundreds of thousands of recruits from conquered villages in Shandong and other northern provinces expanded the ranks of the PLA and local Communist militias. In addition, masses of civilian peasants were forced into combat units to carry supplies and wounded soldiers on the battlefield.

In the late 1940s, Communist troops became better equipped and more disciplined than they had been at the end of World War II.

The PLA quickly learned how to use the heavy weapons they had captured from the Nationalists and inherited from the Soviets. Armed with the big guns of artillery and tanks, Mao's army was no longer limited to the guerrilla-style warfare of ambushes or hit-and-runs. They were now able to launch powerful attacks and plan large-scale offensives.

Chiang's Nationalists fought hard to hold on to their positions, but they found their enemy was only getting stronger. Even after suffering a defeat, the PLA would keep coming back in larger numbers.

As 1947 was coming to an end, Chiang Kai-shek was in a desperate situation. He traveled to the battlefront in southern Manchuria and took personal command in order to restore supply lines to his armies in northern Manchuria.

American military advisers who were still working with Chiang warned him that his forces were spread too thin. They begged him to get his troops out of the northern cities while he still could. They advised him to pull all his troops back to secure the center of China, even if this meant giving up the north. Chiang refused. He knew that whoever controlled Manchuria ultimately controlled all of China. That had been true of the former Manchu emperors, the Japanese, and now the Communists.

Communist marching bands brought victory parades into towns and cities conquered by the People's Liberation Army.

By the spring of 1948, Mao's forces had conquered Yenan again. They were on the march both north and south of the Great Wall. The PLA and their militias destroyed long stretches of railroad and closed in on the three major cities held by the Nationalists in Manchuria: Changchun, the farthest north and most in danger; Mukden, the largest of the three; and Jinzhou, the southernmost city and the lifeline to the rest of China.

Just as Chiang's commanders had feared, the Communists were eventually able to surround the cities altogether, and the Nationalists found themselves trapped and surrounded by hostile locals. Changchun was the first of the three cities to come under siege. In a brutal act that showed how ruthless he could be, Mao Tse-tung ordered the city starved into surrender, resulting in catastrophic civilian deaths.

THE SIEGE OF CHANGCHUN

During the siege of Changchun, the civilian population of 500,000 rapidly ran out of food, and starving people were forced to eat leaves and grass and whatever else they could find. A lucky few were able to escape the city, but more than 200,000 starved to death. A Communist soldier remembered the scene when the PLA entered Changchun after a five-month siege: "When we entered the city, we were devastated. Many of us wept. We're supposed to be fighting for the poor, but of all these dead here, how many are rich? Which of them are Nationalists? Aren't they all poor people?"

61

In October 1948, Lin made his boldest move yet when the PLA attacked Jinzhou and simultaneously cut off 200,000 Nationalist troops in Mukden. Chiang tried to quickly move these troops to help defend Jinzhou, but they were trapped in hostile territory while marching between the two cities, and most of the soldiers were killed or captured.

Of the more than 400,000 troops Chiang had sent north, only about 20,000 made it out alive. Thousands deserted or switched over to the Communists, and tons of American-supplied weapons were seized. The Communists easily captured Mukden on November 1, 1948. They now controlled all of Manchuria, and would quickly control much more.

As bad as it was losing the whole northeastern region of the country, Chiang was suddenly in danger of losing it all. Mao gave his enemy no time to catch his breath. Just five days after Mukden fell, 600,000 PLA troops launched an offensive south from Shandong Province. They moved toward the heart of China and the Nationalist capital of Nanjing. Against them stood a Nationalist army of 550,000. Here the almost evenly matched enemies fought their most decisive battle. It raged between the Huai River and Hai Railroad, and became known as the Battle of Huai-Hai.

The Communists had seized the strategic railroad junction in the city of Suchow, which put their

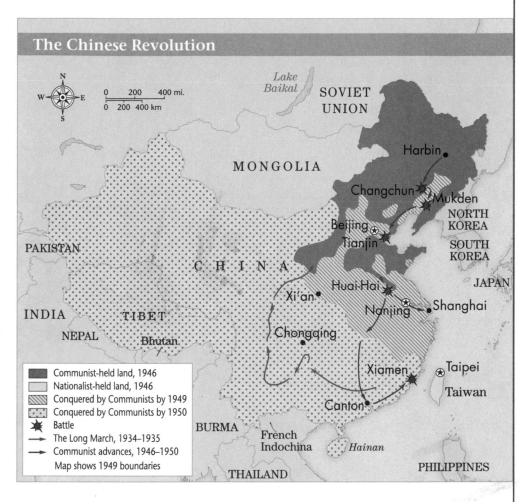

The Chinese Revolution

Lake
Baikal

SOVIET
UNION

MONGOLIA

Harbin

Changchun
Mukden

NORTH
KOREA

Beijing
Tianjin

SOUTH
KOREA

PAKISTAN

C H I N A

JAPAN

Xi'an
Huai-Hai

Nanjing
Shanghai

INDIA

TIBET

Chongqing

NEPAL

Bhutan

Xiamen
Taipei

Taiwan

Canton

BURMA
French
Indochina
Hainan

THAILAND

PHILIPPINES

Communist-held land, 1946
Nationalist-held land, 1946
Conquered by Communists by 1949
Conquered by Communists by 1950
Battle
The Long March, 1934–1935
Communist advances, 1946–1950
Map shows 1949 boundaries

forces right into the middle of Nationalist lines
of defense. With advance knowledge of enemy
movements given to him by a network of spies,
the Communist commander, Chen Yi, was able
to divide Nationalist forces and separate them
into smaller groups. Once they had isolated the
Nationalist forces, the Communists overwhelmed
their enemy with powerful artillery fire and mass
attacks by ground troops.

*The Communists
took major cities as
they surrounded
Nationalist forces.*

63

Troops traveled up the banks of the Huai River during the Battle of Huai-Hai.

During the battle of Huai-Hai, the Communists showed their ability to organize the peasant masses. Millions of peasant civilians participated in this one battle. Swarms of peasant laborers carried ammunition, built fortifications, and dug miles of deep trenches to trap advancing Nationalist tanks.

When it was all over in early January 1949, the entire Nationalist force of more than half a million men had vanished. Many were dead or captured,

but others had deserted or switched sides to the Communists. With Chiang's army eliminated, there was nothing to stop Mao's army from marching to Nanjing and Shanghai, the two centers of Nationalist power. Total Communist victory was now only a matter of time. ◣

Communist Victory

As Nationalist resistance was falling apart during the Battle of Huai-Hai, General Lin Biao's Communist forces swept south from Manchuria and surrounded Beijing, the former capital of the Chinese Empire. Rather than fight a losing battle, the Nationalist commander surrendered the city without resistance. Mao Tse-tung immediately decided to move his capital from Yenan to Beijing, to symbolically establish the CCP as the new rulers of China.

Chiang Kai-shek resigned as Nationalist president but remained in control of the Nationalist Party and whatever armed forces were left. Other Nationalist leaders looked for peace deals with the Communists. There was a proposal to split the country along the Yangtze River, but Mao was long past the point of negotiating. The

Once they gained control of China's cities, CCP commanders had to teach their troops how to operate in urban areas instead of the remote villages they had known.

Communists would settle for nothing less than total victory.

Communist troops rolled into Shanghai without much of a fight and paraded images of their leaders through the streets.

An army of more than 1 million Communists crossed the Yangtze River in April 1949. They captured the Nationalist capital in Nanjing on April 23. Shanghai, China's economic hub, fell

soon after, in May. Throughout the spring and summer, Communists pushed their way south and west into the interior of the country and overwhelmed any remaining opposition. With the sheer power of their numbers, they had become unstoppable.

Chiang Kai-shek and the Nationalists became outlaws in the country they had once ruled. Although he stayed in China for several months, moving from one place to the next, Chiang eventually joined masses of other Nationalists who had already fled to the island of Formosa off China's southeast coast. Here they set up a new Nationalist government and renamed the island Taiwan.

The rapid defeat of the Nationalists came as a surprise to much of the world. Most people at the time knew little about Mao or how powerful his Communists had become in just a few years. In the United States, China was a worse problem than ever for President Truman. He almost lost the 1948 presidential election because of what many saw as his mishandling of the China situation. Truman's government had resumed aid to the Nationalists after General Marshall left the country, but it was too little, too late.

TAIWAN

The large island off China's southeast coast was controlled by the Japanese until the end of World War II, when the Nationalists took over. During the civil war, many Nationalists moved to Taiwan to escape the chaos on the mainland. All told, more than 2 million Nationalists and supporters fled to the island. The Nationalists eventually built a strong economy in Taiwan that exists to this day.

Republican congressmen blasted the Democratic president for his lack of strategy regarding China. The American people wanted to know how the United States could have allowed a country as large and important as China to fall into the hands of the Communists.

Critics argued that the United States should and could have done much more to help the Nationalists defeat the Communists. Some even suggested that the United States use atomic weapons against Mao's forces.

The power of the Soviet Union concerned many people in the United States.

The debate in the United States grew more intense on August 29, 1949, when the Soviet Union shocked the world by testing its first atomic bomb. Cold War tensions were at a peak, and U.S. leaders feared that Communist spies inside the U.S. government had handed over the secret plans for the A-bomb to the Soviets.

With the fearsome Soviet dictator Joseph Stalin in possession of atomic weapons and millions of Chinese coming under control of the Communists, mass hysteria was taking hold of many people in

the United States. Considering the combined forces of the Soviet Union and China, armed with atomic weapons and millions of soldiers, it was easy to imagine that Communists might overrun the entire world.

Americans were worried about Communist enemies among themselves as a "red scare" spread through the country. In the U.S. Congress, the House Un-American Activities Committee had already been investigating suspected Communists for several years. With Mao's forces overrunning China, American diplomats and military figures who had been involved in China came under suspicion. Some were thought to be Communist sympathizers. Others were accused of being spies.

McCarthyism

Anticommunism in the United States in the early years of the Cold War led to a period of American history known as McCarthyism. The era was named for Joseph McCarthy, the U.S. senator from Wisconsin who in 1950 falsely accused U.S. State Department officials of being members of the Communist Party of the United States. McCarthy sat at the head of a Senate committee and spent more than three years investigating people suspected of being underground Communists.

While U.S. officials were being blamed for the defeat of the Nationalists, Chiang Kai-shek could only blame himself. Many U.S. officials were quick to blame him, too.

Chiang had failed to defeat the Communists years earlier when they were weakened and on the run. He had failed to stop the corruption that

In July 1949, Chiang was in Taiwan in exile from the country he once ruled. He never returned to mainland China.

turned people against the Nationalists. He had failed to recognize the overwhelming power of the peasants and do more to gain their support. And he failed to control his military forces, ultimately allowing his armies to be surrounded, trapped, and destroyed.

73

From his new home in Taiwan, Chiang wrote in his diary:

> *This past year has been the darkest and bleakest of my life. ... I have suffered [shame] and defeat.*

Even after his defeat, Chiang Kai-shek still believed he would be victorious in the end. He continued to claim that the Nationalists in Taiwan were the one true government of China. Chiang also vowed that his forces would one day return to the mainland of China and take the country back from the Communists.

By the early fall of 1949, Mao and other top Communist leaders were settled into their new capital in Beijing. On October 1, 1949, CCP leaders gathered to officially announce the establishment of the new government.

During a grand ceremony, Mao formally proclaimed the establishment of the People's Republic of China to a crowd gathered in Tiananmen Square. He spoke from a balcony on top of the main gate to the Forbidden City, the area of Beijing where the emperors once lived. His speech was both short and direct:

> *Now the people's war has been won, and the majority of the people in the country have been liberated.*

Mao went on to list the appointments of key leaders in the new government, with himself as chairman of the Central People's Government. And with that, the one-time outlaw and soon-to-be dictator became ruler of more than one-quarter of the world's people. ◣

Mao Tse tung proclaimed the founding of the People's Republic of China on October 1, 1949.

The Revolution Continues

Chapter

9

Once the Communists were in power, they began transforming China into a communist society. They created plans for a government-controlled economy. They launched massive land reforms. They abolished treaties from China's past that had given special rights to foreign governments and businesses.

At first, the CCP allowed other political parties to have a voice in the new government—except for the Nationalist Party, which was outlawed completely. A new constitution promised personal liberties to China's people. These included freedom of speech and freedom of assembly. The constitution also gave equal rights to women, who had lived as second-class citizens throughout China's history.

Young Chinese Communists were hopeful for the future of the country under Communist rule.

For the Chinese people who had suffered through generations of war and misery, the new government seemed to promise better times to come. But China was headed for a future that for many was even more terrible than its past. In the coming years, China would go through periods of violence and chaos worse than it had ever known.

Large-scale land reforms continued after the CCP extended its control over the entire country. Violence against landlords increased dramatically. In some places, people's trials became mass rallies where thousands of spectators were forced to watch executions. As many as 1 million landowners and their family members were killed in the first few years of Communist rule in China. Countless others were beaten, robbed, and terrorized, until eventually there were no landlords left in China.

There was also trouble brewing on China's borders due to the start of the Korean War. In 1950, Communist North Korea invaded South Korea. The United States was not about to let another country fall to the Communists, so it organized a United Nations military force to come to the aid of South Korea.

KOREAN WAR

The Korean War (1950–1953) was fought to prevent Communists from taking over South Korea. U.N. forces, led by U.S. General Douglas MacArthur, pushed the North Koreans out of South Korea and threatened to conquer North Korea completely. This brought the Chinese into the war on the North Korean side. The war ended in a stalemate, and Korea has been divided into two countries—North Korea and South Korea—ever since.

Mao Tse-tung sent the PLA to support the North Koreans, and they eventually fought the United Nations forces to a stalemate. China's role in the Korean War worsened its relationship with the United States, which continued to support the Nationalists in Taiwan. In fact, the United States refused to recognize the People's Republic of China as a legitimate government.

Throughout the 1950s, the CCP expanded its control over Chinese society, and Mao Tse-tung strengthened his hold on the CCP. Officially, Chou En-lai, the longtime diplomat, was the head of the government as prime minister. But Chairman Mao held the real power.

On December 26, 1950, U.S. Marines in Korea advanced against Communist forces dug into the hillside.

As the Communist revolution continued to transform China, a cult of personality was built around Mao. He became known as the Great Leader, and anyone who questioned his wisdom risked being accused of being an enemy of the people.

Moderate CCP leaders thought there should be a gradual transformation of Chinese society, but Mao demanded a more rapid and radical approach. In 1957, he launched the Great Leap Forward, a program that was meant to modernize China's ancient agricultural system by reorganizing farms and villages into massive communes. Every member of a commune was expected to work for the benefit of the commune and the country as a whole. Before, they had worked for themselves as small farmers.

The Great Leap Forward program was a disaster. It caused mass famine and resulted in as many as 30 million Chinese deaths between 1959 and 1962. By that time, there were still a few CCP leaders brave enough to criticize Mao for his disastrous policy. However, Mao and his supporters responded to any criticism by purging, or removing, critics from the CCP.

The former PLA commander, Lin Biao, became Mao's right-hand man. Lin deepened the cult of personality around Mao. He helped put together a collection of Mao's ideas into a single book, called the *Little Red Book*. It became a sort of sacred text among Mao's worshippers.

In the mid-1960s, Mao launched the Great Cultural Revolution, which was meant to transform Chinese society by destroying the Chinese culture of the past. During the Cultural Revolution, high school and college students were turned into Red Guards. They acted against anyone who may have had a belief in anything except Communist China. Their targets included fellow students, Chinese elders, teachers, and even their parents.

People who represented the old culture of China and who did not fully support Mao and the Communist revolution were targeted by Red Guards. In addition, Mao called on the people to rebel against corrupt members of the Communist Party itself. Lin Biao and the army encouraged and allowed the Red Guards to attack CCP members and others in society.

During the Cultural Revolution, armies of young Red Guards policed their fellow citizens.

81

Millions of people were killed during the Cultural Revolution. People could not speak of their beliefs or opinions. Everyone risked becoming a target of the Red Guards. The madness of the Cultural Revolution was eventually brought to an end as moderate leaders regained control in the early 1970s.

Despite the brutal purges associated with the Cultural Revolution, China's relations with the outside world began to get better. In 1971, the United Nations gave the People's Republic of China a seat on the United Nations Security Council. It had been occupied by the Chinese Nationalist government in Taiwan since the founding of the United Nations. Relations with the United States improved, too, when President Richard Nixon visited China in 1972.

U.S. President Richard Nixon (left) traveled to Beijing in 1972 to meet with Chairman Mao.

82

By then, Mao was nearing the end of his life, and other leaders began to gain control of the CCP. Mao died in 1976 at the age of 82. He survived his old enemy, Chiang Kai-shek, by little more than a year. Chiang controlled the Nationalist government in Taiwan until his death in 1975.

Mao Tse-tung turned out to be a much better revolutionary than national leader. Instead of bringing an end to the chaos that had plagued China's past, he caused more chaos and suffering than the country had ever known. More Chinese ended up being killed during Mao's rule than during all the long years of civil war against the Nationalists.

Only when Mao was gone did China finally begin to awaken from its nightmarish past. Deng Xiaoping, who had been a top commander in the Battle of Huai-Hai, became the new leader of the CCP. Deng and other leaders introduced social and economic reforms that would lead China into the future. Farming communes were dismantled, and peasants were allowed to farm for themselves. Chinese citizens were again allowed to own private property, and economic growth began to turn China into the country we know today.

The relationship between the United States and China has come a long way and is now dominated by the huge amount of trade between the two countries. There are still many tensions, however. The United States continues to support the government in Taiwan and protests China's continued suppression of basic freedoms for its people.

As much as it has changed since the death of Mao Tse-tung, in some ways China is still the same country it has always been. Even with its enormous economic growth, it is still a place where a vast majority of the population are peasant farmers and where only a small percentage of the population reaps the benefits of the growing economy. The Chinese people have few of the freedoms the Communists promised when they seized power in 1949. There is still unrest among the masses. Thousands of protests occur around the country each year, and localized peasant rebellions are common in rural areas.

To this day, the People's Republic of China maintains very tense relations with the Nationalist Chinese government in Taiwan. The United States

TIANANMEN SQUARE

In the spring of 1989, hundreds of thousands of Chinese citizens gathered in Beijing's Tiananmen Square to protest poor economic conditions and corruption within the Communist government. The protesters included students, workers, and people from all walks of life. Government leaders ordered the army to break up the protests, and on June 4, defenseless protesters were massacred by PLA troops using machine guns. As many as 2,000 protesters were killed, and nearly 10,000 were wounded.

remains the main supporter of the Nationalists and continues to supply the government in Taiwan with aid and weapons. Some Nationalists still refuse to recognize the Communists as the legitimate government of China and even threaten to declare independence for Taiwan. The Communist government in Beijing regards Taiwan as a rebellious region and warns that it will reunify China by taking authority over Taiwan—either through peaceful means or by the use of force. Ongoing tensions between these long-standing enemies could one day explode into a new war in China. The Chinese Revolution resulted in Communist triumph, but the end of this conflict may still be yet to come. ◢

The modern skyline of Shanghai displays the economic power of China.

85

Timeline

October 1911

A revolution sweeps through China and overthrows the Chinese Empire.

January 1912

The Republic of China is founded; the Kuomintang (Nationalist Party) is created.

October 1917

The Russian Revolution of 1917 brings Communists to power in Russia.

July 1921

The Chinese Communist Party (CCP) is founded in Shanghai.

1926

Chiang Kai-shek launches the Northern Expedition, which succeeds in defeating China's warlords.

April 1927

The Shanghai Massacre marks the end of the Nationalist-Communist alliance in China.

1931

Japan conquers Manchuria.

1934–1935

Communists retreat across China on the Long March, after which Mao

Tse-tung and the Communists are seen by many as heroes.

1937

Japan invades eastern China and quickly defeats the Nationalist government.

1941

The United States declares war on Japan and becomes allies with both the Nationalists and the CCP.

August 1945

Mao Tse-tung and Chiang Kai-shek meet in Chongqing to discuss peace after Japan surrenders to Allies, and the Soviets invade Manchuria.

November 1945

The Nationalists rout the CCP in southern Manchuria.

December 1945

General George Marshall arrives in China as special representative of President Harry Truman.

January 1946
Marshall secures a cease-fire between Nationalists and Communists.

March 1946
Nationalists launch attacks on Communists as Soviets pull out of Manchuria.

June 1946
Under pressure from Marshall, Chiang agrees to another cease-fire, allowing CCP troops to regroup in northern Manchuria.

July 1946

Nationalists launch new attacks resulting in all-out civil war.

January–April 1947
General Lin Biao's forces launch counterattacks against Nationalists.

April 1947
Nationalists capture CCP capital of Yenan.

January 1948
Chiang takes personal command of forces in Manchuria as Nationalist forces become surrounded in northern cities.

March 1948
Communists retake Yenan.

May–September 1948
Siege of Changchun causes more than 200,000 civilian deaths.

October 1948
Communists conquer Jinzhou, cutting off Nationalist forces farther north.

November 1948
Last Nationalist-held city in Manchuria falls to the Communists, giving them control of the region.

November 1948–January 1949

Battle of Huai-Hai results in the defeat of more than 500,000 Nationalists and leaves China's heartland defenseless against Communist armies.

January 1949
Beijing, the former capital of the Chinese Empire, is surrendered to the Communists; Chiang Kai-shek resigns as president.

April 1949
Nationalist capital in Nanjing falls to the Communists.

Timeline

October 1, 1949

Mao Tse-tung proclaims the People's Republic of China in Beijing.

1950

Chinese Communist forces join North Koreans in the Korean War.

1957

The Great Leap Forward is launched and results in millions of deaths from starvation.

1966

Mao launches the Cultural Revolution, which seeks to destroy traditional Chinese culture.

1972

President Richard Nixon visits China.

1975

Chiang Kai-shek dies.

1976

Mao Tse-tung dies.

ON THE WEB

For more information on this topic, use FactHound.

1 Go to *www.facthound.com*

2 Type in this book ID: 0756520061

3 Click on the *Fetch It* button. FactHound will find the best Web sites for you.

HISTORIC SITES

Chinese American Museum
El Pueblo de Los Angeles
125 Paseo do la Plaza, Suite 400
Los Angeles, CA 90012
(213) 485-8567

This museum shares the history of Chinese Americans through exhibits and educational programs.

LOOK FOR MORE BOOKS IN THIS SERIES

Brown v. Board of Education:
The Case for Integration

The Democratic Party:
America's Oldest Party

The Indian Removal Act:
Forced Relocation

The Japanese American Internment:
Civil Liberties Denied

The Progressive Party:
The Success of a Failed Party

The Republican Party:
The Story of the Grand Old Party

The Scopes Trial:
The Battle Over Teaching Evolution

A complete list of **Snapshots in History** titles is available on our Web site: *www.compasspointbooks.com*

Glossary

alliance
an agreement between nations or groups of people to work together

ambassador
a government official who represents his or her country in a foreign country

artillery
large guns, such as cannons, that require several soldiers to load, aim, and fire

atomic bomb
a weapon that uses nuclear power to create massive destruction

casualties
soldiers killed, captured, missing, or injured during a war

civilians
people not part of a military force

civil war
war between opposing groups within one country

commune
a group of unrelated people or families organized to live together and share everything rather than owning private property

communism
a system in which goods and property are owned by the government and shared in common

Communist
a follower of communism; used specifically to refer to soldiers and members of the Communist Party

cult of personality
extreme adoration or worship of a single leader

democratic
a government system run by officials elected by citizens

empire
a region controlled by an emperor or empress, or a by a single authority

entourage
people who travel with a high-ranking person

guerrillas
soldiers who are not part of a country's regular army and who fight using small, surprise attacks rather than large battles

imperialism
the policy of one country imposing its rule over another country, usually to promote economic interests

liberators
those who free people from captivity or suffering

militias
groups of citizens who have been organized to fight as a group but who are not professional soldiers

Nationalist
someone who has a strong sense of nationalism; used specifically to refer to soldiers and members of the Chinese Nationalist Party

offensive
a military campaign that is organized as a coordinated attack against an opposing force

peasant
a landless farmer who rents farmland from landowners

province
a defined territory within a country that has its own identity, separate from but still a part of the larger country; similar to a state of the United States

refugees
people seeking shelter or refuge, usually driven from their homes by war or other crises

republic
a political system in which officials are elected to represent citizens in government

revolution
drastic change within a short time; also used to describe the overthrow of a government by its own people

skirmishes
small battles

United Nations Security Council
a group of nations that deal with important international issues at the United Nations; the five permanent members of the Security Council are the United States, Russia, China, the United Kingdom, and France

Source Notes

Chapter 1

Page 13, line 11: Jonathan Fenby. *Chiang Kai Shek: China's Generalissimo and the Nation He Lost*. New York: Carroll & Graf Publishers, 2003, p. 455.

Chapter 2

Page 20, line 28: Mao Tse-tung. *Quotations from Chairman Mao Tse-tung*. San Francisco: China Books & Periodicals Inc., 1990, p. 119.

Chapter 3

Page 27, line 1: "China's Communist Revolution, A Glossary." *BBC Online Network*. British Broadcasting Corporation. 18 Sept. 2006. http://news.bbc.co.uk/hi/english/static/special_report/1999/09/99/china_50/long.htm

Chapter 4

Page 36, line 12: Jung Chang and Jon Halliday. *Mao: The Unknown Story*. New York: Alfred A. Knopf, 2005, p. 284.

Chapter 5

Page 42, line 13: *Chiang Kai-shek: China's Generalissimo and the Nation He Lost*, p. 492.

Chapter 6

Page 50, line 4: Jonathan D. Spence. *The Search for Modern China*. New York: W.W. Norton & Co., 1999.

Chapter 7

Page 61, sidebar: *Mao: The Unknown Story*, p. 313.

Chapter 8

Page 74, line 3: *Chiang Kai-shek: China's Generalissimo and the Nation He Lost*, p. 495.

Page 7, line 25: Mao Tse-tung. Public Speech. "Proclamation of the Central People's Government of the People's Republic of China, Beijing, China." 1 Oct. 1949.

SELECT BIBLIOGRAPHY

Chang, Jung. *Wild Swans: Three Daughters of China.* New York: Simon & Schuster, 2003.

Chang, Jung and Halliday, Jon. *Mao: The Unknown Story.* New York: Alfred A. Knopf, 2005.

Fairbanks, John King. *The Great Chinese Revolution: 1800–1985.* New York: HarperCollins, 1986.

Fenby, Jonathan. *Chiang Kai-shek: China's Generalissimo and the Nation He Lost.* New York: Carroll & Graf Publishers, 2003.

Meisner, Maurice. *Mao's China: A History of the People's Republic.* New York: The Free Press, 1999.

Salisbury, Harrison E. *China: 100 Years of Revolution.* New York: Holt, Rinehart and Winston, 1983.

Salisbury, Harrison E. *The Long March: The Unknown Story.* New York: Harper & Row, 1985.

Spence, Jonathan D. *The Search for Modern China.* New York: W.W. Norton & Co., 1999.

Tse-tung, Mao. *Quotations from Chairman Mao Tse-tung.* San Francisco: China Books & Periodicals Inc., 1990.

Tuchman, Barbara. *Stilwell and the American Experience in China.* New York: The Macmillan Company, 1970.

FURTHER READING

Hatt, Christine. *Mao Zedong.* Milwaukee: World Almanac Library, 2004.

Malaspina, Ann. *The Chinese Revolution and Mao Zedong in World History.* Berkeley Heights, N.J.: Enslow Publishers, 2004.

Pietrusza, David. *The Chinese Cultural Revolution.* San Diego: Lucent Books, 1996.

Yu, Chun. *Little Green: Growing Up During the Chinese Cultural Revolution.* New York: Simon & Schuster Books for Young Readers, 2005.

Index

ABOUT THE AUTHOR

Paul J. Byrne is a writer and editor from Connecticut. He holds a degree in history and economics. Paul writes about people, history, and the natural world and has worked on a number of children's publications. He lives with his wife, Marina, and daughter, Stella, in Stratford, Connecticut.

IMAGE CREDITS